MY FIRST BOOK
SOUTH AFRICA

D1502189

ALL ABOUT SOUTH AFRICA FOR KIDS

GL●BED
CHILDREN BOOKS

Interior and cover Design: Daniel Day
Editor: Margaret Bam

For My Sons, Daniel, David and Jude

Cape Town Harbour, South Africa

South Africa

South Africa is a **country**.

A country is land that is controlled by a **single government**. Countries are also called **nations, states, or nation-states**.

Countries can be **different sizes**. Some countries are big and others are small.

Drakensberg Amphitheatre, South Africa

Where Is South Africa?

South Africa is located in the continent of **Africa**.

A continent is **a massive area of land that is separated from others by water or other natural features**.

South Africa is situated in **Southern** Africa.

Cape Town, South Africa

Capital

The capitals of South Africa are Pretoria, Cape Town and Bloemfontein.

Cape Town is located in the **south-western part** of the country.

Johannesburg is the largest city in South Africa.

South Africa coast

Provinces

South Africa is divided into nine provinces

The provinces of South Africa are as follows

North West, Northern Cape, Gauteng, Limpopo, Mpumalanga, Free State, KwaZulu-Natal, Eastern Cape and Western Cape.

Population

South Africa has a population of around **60 million people** making it the 5th most populated country in Africa and the 24th most populated country in the world.

Johannesburg, South Africa

Size

South Africa is **1,221,037 square kilometres** making it the 24th largest country in the world by area. South Africa is the 9th largest country in Africa.

Languages

The official languages of South Africa are **Zulu, Xhosa, Afrikaans, English, Sepedi, Swazi, Sesotho, Setswana, Xitsonga, Tshivenda and Ndebele.**

There are other languages spoken in South Africa such as **Fanagalo, Khoe and Lobedu.**

Here are a few ways to say welcome
- **Wamukelekile - Zulu**
- **Wamkelekile - Xhosa**
- **Welkom - Afrikaans**

Addo Elephant National Park

Attractions

There are lots of interesting places to see in South Africa.

Some beautiful places to visit in South Africa are

- **Kruger National Park**
- **Kirstenbosch National Botanical Garden**
- **Apartheid Museum**
- **Sun City Resort**
- **V&A Waterfront**
- **Addo Elephant National Park**

Blyde River Canyon, Mpumalanga, South Africa

History of South Africa

People have lived in South Africa for a very long time. In fact, South Africa is home to some of the oldest human-fossil sites in the world. These finds suggest that various hominid species existed in the area as far back as three million years ago.

The Khoikhoi and San were the original inhabitants of present-day South Africa.

South Africa gained independence from the United Kingdom on 31st May 1961.

Xhosa woman

Customs in South Africa

South Africa has many fascinating customs and traditions.

- **The Xhosa people of South Africa are known for their beautiful and complex dressing that portrays a person's social status, position in the society, and whether they are married or not.**
- **Some South Africans follow a hierarchical sequence in the order of people served: guests first, followed by the eldest male, remaining men, children and, lastly, women.**

Music of South Africa

There are many different music genres in South Africa such as **Kwela Music, Kwaito, Amapiano, Mbaqanga, Jazz, Gqom, Marabi and Isicathamiya.**

Some notable South African musicians include
- **Mafikizolo**
- **Black Coffee**
- **Abdullah Ibrahim**
- **Kabza De Small**
- **Master KG**

Food of South Africa

South African food is known for being tasty, delicious and flavoursome.

The national dish of South Africa is **Bobotie** which is a dish made with meat, dried fruits, and herbs, topped with milk and egg mixture.

Braai meat

Food of South Africa

Some popular dishes in South Africa include

- Braai
- Vetkoek
- Boerewors
- Bobotie
- Biltong
- Potjiekos
- Durban bunny chow

The City Hall in Durban, South Africa

Weather in South Africa

South Africa has a varied climate ranging from **desert and semi-desert in the northwest to subtropical on the eastern coast.** South Africa has four seasons—summer, fall, winter, and spring.

The warmest month in South Africa is January.

Small monkey in South Africa

Animals of South Africa

There are many wonderful animals in South Africa.

Here are some animals that live in South Africa

- Lion
- Elephant
- Rhinoceros
- African buffalo
- Cheetah
- Hippo

Kruger National Park

National Parks

There are many beautiful national parks in South Africa which is one of the reasons why so many people visit this beautiful country every year.

Here are some of South Africa's national parks

- Kruger National Park
- Addo Elephant National Park
- Marakele National Park
- Golden Gate Highlands National Park

South Africa soccer fans

Sports in South Africa

Sports play an integral part in South African culture. The most popular sports are **soccer, rugby, and cricket.**

Here are some of famous sportspeople from South Africa

- **Gary Player - Golf**
- **Benni McCarthy - Football**
- **Hansie Cronje - Cricket**
- **Ernie Els - Golf**
- **Francois Pienaar - Rugby**

The Statue of Nelson Mandela, Pretoria

Famous

Many successful people hail from South Africa.

Here are some notable South African figures

- **Charlize Theron – Actress**
- **Nelson Mandela – Head of State**
- **Desmond Tutu – Bishop**
- **Thabo Mbeki – Politician**
- **Steve Biko - Activist**

Woman in South African Market

Something Extra...

As a little something extra, we are going to share some lesser known facts about South Africa

- **South Africa is the largest producer of macadamia nuts in the world.**
- **South Africa is home to the largest visible crater in the world.**

Camps Bay, Cape Town, South Africa

Words From the Author

We hope that you enjoyed learning about the wonderful country of South Africa.

South Africa is a country rich in culture and beauty, with lots of wonderful places to visit and people to meet.

We hope you continue to learn more about this wonderful nation. If you enjoyed this book, consider leaving a review!

With Love

Made in United States
North Haven, CT
14 March 2023